COWBOYS AT THE BALLET

The Story of Choreographer Agnes de Mille

Claire Wrenn Bobrow

Illustrated by Ilaria Urbinati

ATHENEUM BOOKS FOR YOUNG READERS
New York Amsterdam/Antwerp London Toronto Sydney/Melbourne New Delhi

ATHENEUM BOOKS FOR YOUNG READERS • An imprint of Simon & Schuster Children's Publishing Division • 1230 Avenue of the Americas, New York, New York 10020 • For more than 100 years, Simon & Schuster has championed authors and the stories they create. By respecting the copyright of an author's intellectual property, you enable Simon & Schuster and the author to continue publishing exceptional books for years to come. We thank you for supporting the author's copyright by purchasing an authorized edition of this book. • No amount of this book may be reproduced or stored in any format, nor may it be uploaded to any website, database, language-learning model, or other repository, retrieval, or artificial intelligence system without express permission. All rights reserved. Inquiries may be directed to Simon & Schuster, 1230 Avenue of the Americas, New York, NY 10020 or permissions@simonandschuster.com. • Text © 2026 by Claire Wrenn Bobrow • Illustration © 2026 by Ilaria Urbinati • Book design by Karyn Lee • All rights reserved, including the right of reproduction in whole or in part in any form. • ATHENEUM BOOKS FOR YOUNG READERS is a registered trademark of Simon & Schuster, LLC. Atheneum logo is a trademark of Simon & Schuster, LLC. • For information about special discounts for bulk purchases, please contact Simon & Schuster Special Sales at 1-866-506-1949 or business@simonandschuster.com. • Simon & Schuster strongly believes in freedom of expression and stands against censorship in all its forms. For more information, visit BooksBelong.com. • The Simon & Schuster Speakers Bureau can bring authors to your live event. For more information or to book an event, contact the Simon & Schuster Speakers Bureau at 1-866-248-3049 or visit our website at www.simonspeakers.com. • The text for this book was set in Scotch Modern. • The illustrations for this book were rendered digitally. • Manufactured in China • 1125 SCP • First Edition • 10 9 8 7 6 5 4 3 2 1 • Library of Congress Cataloging-in-Publication Data • Names: Bobrow, Claire Wrenn, author. | Urbinati, Ilaria, 1984- illustrator. • Title: Cowboys at the ballet : the story of choreographer Agnes de Mille / Claire Wrenn Bobrow ; illustrated by Ilaria Urbinati. • Description: First edition. | New York : Atheneum Books for Young Readers, 2026. | Audience: Ages 4-8 | Summary: "A spirited picture book about the epic struggle and dramatic breakthrough of Agnes de Mille, the legendary American choreographer of Oklahoma and Carousel whose work changed the course of Broadway history"—Provided by publisher. • Identifiers: LCCN 2024037570 (print) | LCCN 2024037571 (ebook) | ISBN 9781665957878 (hardcover) | ISBN 9781665957885 (ebook) • Subjects: LCSH: De Mille, Agnes—Juvenile literature. | Dancers—United States—Biography—Juvenile literature. | Choreographers—United States—Biography—Juvenile literature. • Classification: LCC GV1785.D36 B63 2026 (print) | LCC GV1785.D36 (ebook) | DDC 792.8/092 [B]—dc23/eng/20250115 •
LC record available at https://lccn.loc.gov/2024037570 • LC ebook record available at https://lccn.loc.gov/2024037571

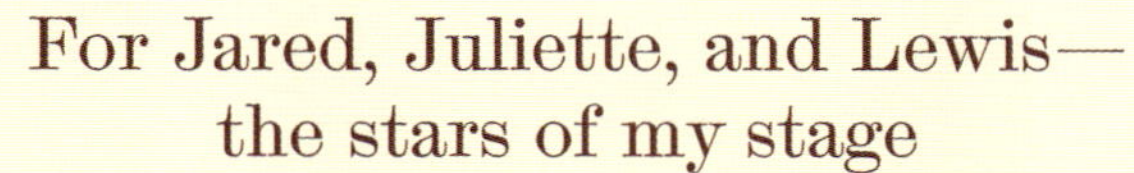

For Jared, Juliette, and Lewis—
the stars of my stage

—C. W. B.

This book is dedicated to Dora,
who is a young ballerina and a passionate reader,
and to all the creative and brave young women
who follow their dreams no matter what

—I. U.

Lights dim.
Whispers hush.
Excitement crackles through the crowd.
Something new is about to happen on this famous stage,
something extraordinary.
Tonight, after a long, hard road . . .
there will be cowboys at the ballet.

In a dusty California town awash with dreams,
where cowboys roam and rattlesnakes slither,
a girl grows amid ocean breezes and orange groves,
sagebrush and sky.

Her name is Agnes de Mille,
and she longs to be a dancer.

When ballet lessons begin,
Agnes stretches and strains her body
but struggles to master the techniques.
Yet her brain bubbles
with characters and stories,
which flow into her footwork.

She creates her own unique dances
to perform for family, friends, and schoolmates,
about mythology,
a couple at a picnic,
ballerinas struck with stage fright.

Her audiences giggle and gasp,
grimace and guffaw!

The characters are funny, real, familiar—
nothing at all like the ones in classical ballet.

So Agnes gallops ahead,
chasing her dream to New York,
following her passion.
She bucks and snorts with energy
and ideas—just like America!

In the wake of World War I,
the nation revels in a sense of pride,
prosperity, and freedom.

Traditions and rules clatter to the ground
like rusty nails.
American artists turn to
their own country for inspiration,
celebrating ordinary life and everyday people,
putting the real above the ideal.

Agnes flings herself into this seething stampede of creativity. But with no major dance companies or training schools to guide her, there's no obvious way forward.

Agnes must forge her own path.

She keeps creating,
performing a show here, a dance there.
Inventing as she goes, combining old steps
with new ones based on honest emotion,
Agnes explores the artistic frontier.

Yet no one knows what to make of Agnes de Mille.
She's not a classical dancer,
or a modern dancer,
or a folk dancer.

What is she?

Then one day a teacher sees her perform and catches a spark of something special. She invites Agnes to train in London. Agnes leaps at the chance!

She studies choreography,
mixing a bit of ballet,
a fragment of folk,
a morsel of modern,
weaving in everyday, ordinary gestures:
a pout instead of a pirouette,
eating a sandwich instead of angling into an arabesque.

Again and again, people applaud,
but no one begs for more.

Agnes still doesn't fit the mold.
She's stuck.

Then one summer, while visiting Colorado,
Agnes attends a rodeo.
The cowboys fascinate her, how they ride and rope.
She studies their movements,
feels their power, strength, and nerve.

It’s almost like dancing.
And they remind her of home . . .
of ocean breezes and orange groves,
sagebrush and sky,
of wide-open spaces and limitless potential.

She stores away the memories and keeps creating, performing a show here, a dance there.

People start to say her work has "the de Mille touch."

She's asked to make dances for a film, a play, and then . . .

a Broadway musical. Hooray!

But the show opens—
and fails.

Agnes stumbles away feeling just like the title: *Hooray for What!*

Back in damp, dreary London, Agnes slumps.
Where had her trail gone cold?
She thinks back to the beginning,
to a dusty town awash with dreams,
to a long-ago rodeo.

To thunderous hoofbeats, twirling ropes,
and . . . cowboys.

Agnes can almost feel the horse beneath her
as she looks at the London sky.

Slowly but surely, she picks herself up
and creates a new short piece—
Rodeo.

She teaches a group of dancers to move
like cowboys out on the range,
then puts on a show.

It's strange and new and wonderful.
Now audiences and critics applaud—
and beg for more!

At last the freedom to experiment has put Agnes on the right trail.

But as she finally sits tall in the saddle,
a thunderclap shakes the world.
War.
Agnes is forced to leave London.

Back in America, opportunities to dance dry up faster than watering holes in the desert.

Days and weeks pass,

then months.

And years.

Weary and discouraged, Agnes wants to quit.

Then, out of the clear blue sky,
a ballet company comes looking for something fresh to perform—
a dance that will speak to the spirit of a nation,
to the wartime mood of nostalgia, strength, and pride.

Its audiences yearn for something new, something American,
something . . . Agnes?

Yeehaw! She leaps back in the saddle, turning *Rodeo* into a full-length ballet.

It becomes the story of a plucky, misfit cowgirl—a bit like Agnes herself.

She plants her heels and digs in, teaching classically trained dancers to hitch up their britches and move like they've been riding and roping all their lives.

This isn't ballet! holler the dancers, confused. But they soon stretch and sway as if real horses thunder beneath them.

Finally it is opening night.
Dancers shift in the wings,
ready to step into the spotlight—
Agnes among them.
Lights dim.
Whispers hush.

Excitement crackles through the crowd.
Something new is about to happen on this famous stage,
something extraordinary.
After a long, hard road, at last . . .

there are cowboys at the ballet.

AUTHOR'S NOTE

Agnes George de Mille (1905–1993) was an American original. Raised in the heady atmosphere of early Hollywood, she drank up the drive and creativity that flourished in those dry hills and used it to make her own starry yet hard-won ascent—not in the movies but in the world of dance. She was smitten by the art form, thanks to ballerina and global sensation Anna Pavlova, and inspired by family members who had achieved mythic status in their own fields, including her uncle, the movie director Cecil B. DeMille. Agnes set her heart on becoming a dancer and strived for greatness—nothing less would do. But despite her privileged upbringing, it did not come easy. She started dance training late, at age fourteen, due to family opposition. And though she devoted herself to rigorous practice at home, Agnes's formal lessons were infrequent and her body type defied convention, causing her further significant challenges. Success was a long time coming. Yet Agnes refused to quit.

Her legendary contributions to the world of dance and choreography finally took flight when she was thirty-seven years old at the premiere of *Rodeo* (pronounced row-DAY-oh) on the stage of the Metropolitan Opera House in New York City. Agnes herself danced the lead role of the Cowgirl. And after the last whoopin', stompin' footfall, the cast received an astonishing twenty-two curtain calls. It was a smash hit! After years of struggle, Agnes had finally made her mark and started a revolution along the way—in ballet, Broadway musicals, and beyond.

Thanks to *Rodeo*, Agnes went on to choreograph many other ballets, as well as some of the most famous musicals in Broadway history, including *Oklahoma!*, *One Touch of Venus*, *Carousel*, *Gentlemen Prefer Blondes*, and *Brigadoon*. Her distinctly American style and innovative approach, based on honest emotions and ordinary gestures, were integral to the overall storytelling and helped drive the narratives. Audiences and critics found her work captivating.

But Agnes did not stop with success on Broadway. She went on to become a brilliant author, an innovative television presenter, the leader of several dance companies, and a fierce advocate for government funding of the arts. Her energy was tireless, her spirit indomitable.

She embodied her mother's admonition to "do something!" and the only thing that stopped her was her death at the age of eighty-eight.

Among her many accomplishments, Agnes was the first female choreographer/director of a Broadway musical, one of the first women to lead a national labor union, the winner of two Tonys and an Emmy Award, and the recipient of New York City's Handel Medallion (the city's highest civilian honor); a Kennedy Center Honor; and, in 1986, the National Medal of Arts—the highest arts-related award given by the government of the United States. In addition, she was a founding member of American Ballet Theatre; wrote numerous highly acclaimed books about her life and the art and history of dance; and was a significant contributor to educational television programs, including the *Omnibus* series and *Conversations About the Dance*, bringing knowledge of dance into the homes of millions of Americans for the very first time.

In her long and illustrious life, Agnes de Mille captured not only the spirit of a cowgirl but the heart of a nation.

Selected Sources

Acocella, Joan. "Agnes de Mille's Artistic Justice." *New Yorker*, November 5, 2015.

Agnes de Mille's Dances. "Rodeo: The Courting at Burnt Ranch." De Mille Working Group. https://www.agnesdemille.com/test-blog-gallery/2019/7/24/rodeo.

de Mille, Agnes. *Dance to the Piper*. New York: The New York Review of Books, 1951.

Easton, Carol. *No Intermissions: The Life of Agnes de Mille*. New York: Little, Brown and Company, 1996.

Gardner, Kara Anne. *Agnes de Mille: Telling Stories in Broadway Dance*. New York: Oxford University Press, 2016.

Gaskill, Rachel. *The Library of American Choreographers: Agnes de Mille*. New York: Rosen Publishing Group, 2006.

Speaker-Yuan, Margaret. *American Women of Achievement: Agnes de Mille, Choreographer*. New York: Chelsea House, 1990.